DEPRESSION

BITE SIZED BIBLE STUDIES

What To Do When You Feel Blue

God's Word For
Depression & Discouragement

6 SESSIONS

BETH JONES

When your words came, I ate them;
they were my joy and my heart's delight . . .
Jeremiah 15:16 NIV

The Bite Sized Bible Study Series Includes . . .

- Satisfied Lives For Desperate Housewives: God's Word On Proverbs 31
- Kissed or Dissed: God's Word For Feeling Rejected & Overlooked
- Grace For The Pace: God's Word For Stressed & Overloaded Lives
- Don't Factor Fear Here: God's Word For Overcoming Anxiety, Fear & Phobias
- The Friends God Sends: God's Word On Friendship & Chick Chat
- What To Do When You Feel Blue: God's Word For Depression & Discouragement

Beth Jones is a Bible teacher, author, wife and mother of four children who ministers the Word of God in a relevant and inspiring way by sharing down-to-earth insights. She is the author of the popular Bible study series *Getting A Grip On The Basis* which is being used by thousands of churches in America and abroad, *Why The Gory, Bloody Details?*, and the *Bite Sized Bible Study Series*. Beth also writes a bi-weekly newspaper column titled *"Just Us Girls"* and hosts www.bethjones.org. She and her husband Jeff founded and serve as the senior pastors of Kalamazoo Valley Family Church.

Beth Jones may be reached @
Kalamazoo Valley Family Church, 269.324.5599
www.bethjones.org or www.kvfc.org

DEPRESSION

BITE SIZED BIBLE STUDIES

What To Do When You Feel Blue

God's Word For
Depression & Discouragement

6 SESSIONS

BETH JONES

Valley Press Publishers
Portage, MI

valleypresspublishers.com

What To Do When You Feel Blue
God's Word For Depression & Discouragement
ISBN: 1-933433-00-0

Copyright © 2005 Beth Ann Jones

Published by Valley Press Publishers - A Ministry of KVFC
995 Romence Road, Portage, MI 49024
800-596-0379   www.kvfc.org

Printed in the United States of America.
ALL RIGHTS RESERVED.

Contents

Acknowledgments

Writing a book is like having a baby! I've been "pregnant" with many books over the years and have found that once a book is "conceived" by the Holy Spirit and begins to grow, the gestation period can range from a few years to several decades. Then it seems that at the right time, when I'm "full-term" and "great with child", the Lord puts an "urge" to write within me which eventually triggers the labor pains, transition and ultimately the birth of a book! It takes a lot of people to give birth to a book and I'd like to honor those the Lord has put in my life to coach, pray, support and encourage me in these writing endeavors.

First, my husband, Jeff. You have been my best friend and most consistent encourager. When I have been uncertain, you've always been rock solid and gone the extra mile to help me fulfill God's will in writing. Thanks for loving me and believing in God's call on my life.

Second, my children, Meghan, Annie, Luke and Eric. I've had to take more time away to write; thanks for being understanding and willing to let mom go. I couldn't have asked for four better children. I love you all.

Third, my mom. What an inspiration you have always been to me! Thanks for letting me hang out with you in Florida to write these books.

Fourth, our staff. Our Associate Publisher, April Wedel, our Editorial Coordinator, Juli DeGraaf and our Publications Coordinator, Joanne Davis. I appreciate your love, faith, heart to get the Word out and the long hours you have spent helping me give birth to this book! I also want to thank the entire KVFC staff for their love, support and encouragement.

Fifth, all the volunteer copy editors and pray-ers. A very special thanks to Mary VanderWal, Carol Lacey and Elise Burch for your time, comments and editing help. I especially appreciate my dear praying friends Mary VanderWal, Mary Jo Fox, Kate Cook, Cindy Boester, Jennifer Nederhoed, Pam Roe-Vanderberg, Jennifer Palthe, Colleen DeBruin, Molly Nicolai, KVFC prayer teams and many others who have continually lifted me and these projects to the Lord in prayer.

Sixth, Pat Judd, Bryan Norris and all the guys with CrossStaff. Thanks for partnering with us in this project. Let's have fun watching what the Lord will do!

I love God's Word. I don't just like it; I love it. It's more valuable to me than anything. If I had to spend the rest of my life on a remote, uninhabited island and could only take one thing, I would take my Bible. Why? It's simple. God has changed and upgraded every area of my life as I have simply read, believed and obeyed the Bible.

It wasn't always that way. Like many people, I had never even considered reading the Bible for myself, much less studying it. The Bible was for priests, theologians and monks. It was not relevant to my life. It was a dusty old book in our basement. One day, when I was about 14 years old, I just got the "urge" to read the Bible. I started with Genesis, and within the first few chapters I fell asleep. That was the end of my Bible reading.

It wasn't until five years later when I was a 19-year-old college freshman that my roommate began to share with me what the Bible said about God, about life and about me. I was shocked at the "living" quality of the Bible. It wasn't like any other book I read. This wasn't like reading the president's biography. This wasn't like reading the dull Western Civilization textbooks in front of me. It was as if God Himself was explaining the contents to me. Something was happening in my heart as I read God's Word. I was challenged. I was encouraged. I was comforted. The Living God was speaking through His Living Word. During this time I developed a hunger for God and His Word. I stayed up late to read the Bible. I pondered it during the day. There was plenty I didn't understand, but I received strength, energy and wisdom just by reading it, and ultimately the Holy Spirit drew me to Jesus.

As a new Christian in my sophomore year of college, my Bible study leader simply exhorted me to read my Bible a lot and "let the Word of Christ dwell richly inside of me." It was the best advice ever! The result was that I began to develop an insatiable appetite for God's Word and a passionate desire to share God's Word with others. As I read my Bible, Jesus walked off the pages and came to live in my heart. Jesus isn't just alive in heaven, He is alive to me. I've come to know Him intimately through fellowship with Him in His Word.

Isn't it great that God's Word is interactive—not just historic or static? God's Word is living and active and able to effectually work within us to affect change and impart the miraculous! The Bible is the most amazing book ever! It has been banned, burned and blasted, but it lives on and continues to be the world's best-selling book.

Unfortunately, I have found that lots of people just don't understand the Bible and as a result, they get overwhelmed, bored or frustrated. Many Christians have never really tasted the rich, daily, life-changing flavor of God's Word. If you want to grow and mature in God, you have to "eat" large quantities of the Word. Once you taste and see that the Lord and His Word are good, nothing else will satisfy you! Think of it this way: if all you've ever tasted are peanut butter and jelly sandwiches, then you are pretty content with a good PBJ. But the minute you taste a filet mignon, you can never again be satisfied by a PBJ. In some ways, I have found that is the story for many Christians. If you're one of those people that have been content with a spiritual PBJ, I've got good news for you; get your taste buds ready for some rich, tasty, "meaty" morsels from God's Word. The more you eat it, the better it tastes!

Our goal in the Bite Sized Bible Study Series is to create an addiction in you for Bible study, and more importantly for knowing God intimately through the revelation knowledge of His Word, by His Spirit. As you explore these studies, I believe that the Holy Spirit will speak to your heart and transmit the supernatural revelation you need to operate victoriously in this life.

Jeremiah was right:

"When your words came, I ate them;
they were my joy and my heart's delight . . ."
Jeremiah 15:16, NIV

May this be your testimony, too!

This Bible study can be used individually as well as in small groups. It's ideal for those who are hungry to learn from the Word, but who have a limited amount of time to meet together with others.

The Bite Sized Bible Study Series is designed for all types of Bible study formats.

- Individual Study
- Women's Small Groups
- Lunchtime Study at Work
- Neighborhood Bible Study
- Couples Small Groups
- Sunday School Class
- Prison Ministry
- Student and Youth Small Groups
- Outreach Bible Study
- Early Morning Men's Bible Groups
- Singles Small Groups
- Recovery and Felt Need Groups

For Individual Study

Pray. Ask God, by the Holy Spirit, to customize these sessions for you personally.

Expect. Turn your "expectation" on and trust God to speak to your heart.

Dive. Grab your Bible, pen and favorite beverage and dive in!

For Small Group Study Leaders

Pray. Ask God, by the Holy Spirit, to reveal and customize these sessions for you and your group members.

Expect. Turn your "expectation" on and trust God to speak to your heart, as well as the hearts of those in your small group.

Facilitate. Small groups will do better with a facilitator, preferably a more mature Christian who can add helpful comments as well as lead a heartfelt time of prayer before and after each session. It's important that you keep things moving in the right direction. As the leader of the small group, keep in mind that it's your job to facilitate discussion and not act as the "teacher" who does all the talking. It's important for those in the group to verbalize their discoveries, so do your best to create an atmosphere where each member feels free to share what they are learning from God's Word.

Encourage. Encourage everyone to participate. Help those who talk a lot to take a breather and let others share their insights as well.

Focus. Stay focused on God the Father, Jesus, and the Holy Spirit Who gave us the Scriptures. Our goal is to see what God has said in His Word. Keep in mind that this is a Bible study and not a place for "my opinion" or "my church believes" or "here's what I think" comments. Always direct people's attention back to the Bible to see what the Scriptures say.

Highlight. Hit the high points. If you face time constraints, you may not have enough time to cover every detail of each lesson. As the leader, prayerfully prepare and be sure you cover the highlights of each session.

Digest. We've endeavored to "cut up" the Word through this Bite Sized Bible Study, and as a leader it's your job to help those in your small group digest the Scriptures so they can benefit from all the spiritual nutrition in each word.

Discuss. Take time to answer the three discussion questions at the end of each Bible study session. These should help stimulate heartfelt conversation.

If you want this Bible study to really impact your life, you must be certain of one major thing: you must be certain you are a Christian according to God's definition and instruction in the Bible. You must be certain that you are accepted by God; that you are saved. So let's begin our study by considering this important issue.

Did you know that some people want to be a Christian on their terms, rather than on God's terms? Sometimes people want to emphasize church, religion and their goodness as evidence of their Christianity. For some, it will be a rude awakening to discover that the Bible tells us God isn't impressed by any of those substitutes. Did you know that God isn't interested in our denominational tags? He's not wowed by our church membership pedigree, either. He's not moved by our good deeds and benevolent accomplishments. The thing that most impresses God is His Son, Jesus Christ. *"For God so loved the world that he gave his one and only Son, that whoever believes in him shall not perish but have eternal life."* *John 3:16, NIV* God paid quite a price to send His own Son to the cross to pay the penalty for our sin. It's really an insult to Him to trust in or substitute anything or anyone else for Jesus Christ. The key to being a Christian is to believe in, trust, receive and confess Jesus Christ as your Lord and Savior.

Why would you or anyone want to believe in, trust, receive and confess Jesus Christ as Lord? Why would you want to know Jesus personally and to be known by Him? Unless you truly understand your condition before God, you wouldn't have any reason to! However, when you realize the magnitude of your sin—those private and public thoughts, deeds, actions and words that you and God know about—when you listen to your conscience and realize that truly "all have sinned," including you, it can be very sobering. It's even more sobering to realize that according to God's justice system, *". . . the wages of sin is death . . ."* *Romans 6:23 NKJV* It's a big wake up call when it really hits you that the consequence of sin is death. Death which is defined as an eternal separation from God is the payment you will receive for your sin. When you realize your true, hopeless, lost condition before God, you will run to Him in order to be saved. This reality causes people to quit playing religious games and to quit trusting in their own works of righteousness. Our lost condition forces us to forgo being "churchy" or "religious", apathetic, passive and indifferent, and to become hungry for the Merciful Living God. It's good news to discover that " . . . *the gift of God is eternal life in Christ Jesus our Lord." Romans 6:23 NKJV*

What does God require of us? The qualification for eternal life is simply to believe on Jesus. Many people say they believe in God or in Jesus Christ. In fact, the Bible tells us that the devil himself believes and trembles. According to the Bible, God's definition of a Christian believer—or a Christ One—is the person who believes in their heart that God raised Jesus from the dead and who confesses with his or her mouth that Jesus Christ is their Lord. In other words, their heart and mouth agree that Jesus is Lord! We see this in Romans 10:13, 9, *". . . whoever calls on the name of the LORD shall be saved . . . if you confess with your mouth the Lord Jesus and believe in your heart that God has raised Him from the dead, you will be saved." NKJV*

This is something we do on purpose. It's a sobering thought to consider that if you've never purposely repented of your sin and invited Jesus Christ to be the Lord of your life, you may not be saved—you may not be a Christian according to God's definition. Would you like to be certain that you are a Christian; that you have a relationship with the Lord and eternal salvation? It's simple, just answer these questions: Do you believe that God raised Jesus from the dead? Will you give Him the steering wheel of your life and trust Him to forgive all your sins and make you an entirely new person? Will you trust Jesus Christ alone to save you? Are you willing to invite Him into your life and will you confess that He is your Lord? If so, please pray this prayer from your heart. God will hear you, Jesus Christ will forgive your sins and enter your life. You will be a Christian.

"Dear God, I come to you as a person who recognizes my condition before you. I see that I am a sinner in need of a Savior. Jesus, I do believe that God raised You from the dead and I now invite you into my life. I confess Jesus as my Lord. I want to know You and be the Christian You have called me to be, according to Your definition. I thank You, in Jesus' Name. Amen."

Got the blues? Bummed out? In the dumps? Have you experienced a setback or disappointment lately? Grieving a loss? Heavy-hearted? Down? Gloomy? Feel isolated, overlooked, rejected? Do you frequently attend pity parties? Have your sleeping and eating habits changed? Felt detached, confused or apathetic? Does your situation feel hopeless? Want to run away? While your friends are reaching higher toward their dreams and desires, do you feel like you're reaching a new low? Ever felt like the sky of your life was gray? What do you do when the sky is not blue? These are all signs and symptoms of depression and discouragement and we've all been there in one way or another.

Maybe you're tired of being down, sad or dependent on mood-enhancing drugs or herbs. Perhaps you wonder if God has real answers. The good news for each of us is that God cares and He has real answers to help us.

Depression is a big problem these days. Whether it's clinical depression or severe depression, many people are unable to cope with daily life without the help of prescription drugs or intoxication. It doesn't seem to matter whether you're a teen or adult, male or female, single, married, or a parent; everyone is tempted at times to get down. If you've been severely depressed, kind of down in the dumps or just have a mild case of the blues, this study will be encouraging to you.

How I Learned This Lesson

The "mentals and the bluks": that is how I described a season of the blues during my junior year in college. I was

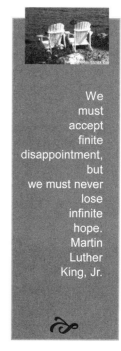

We must accept finite disappointment, but we must never lose infinite hope.
Martin Luther King, Jr.

a nice, "happy-go-lucky," Christian college student with plans to become a dentist. I had just spent 12 weeks with a campus ministry on a summer project in New Hampshire. It was a life-changing time of beach evangelism and growing in my faith. I returned to college as a junior and was on fire, sold out, ready to serve God with my life! In the first few months of that school year, I had a dramatic encounter with the Lord where He called me to the ministry, quickened Romans 10:13-15 to my heart and gave me a "mini-vision" of what I'd be doing someday. This period of 4-6 months was a marked time in my personal destiny. I was excited about God and I wanted to spend my life doing eternal things.

Little did I know that the enemy would immediately try to quench my zeal and commitment to God. My "happy-go-lucky" disposition was attacked and I found myself feeling depressed, bummed out and frustrated. I didn't quite know what it was. I remember telling my Bible study leader that I felt the "mentals and the bluks." The only way I could describe it was that it seemed that negative thoughts were bombarding my mind and I felt blue for no specific reason. I eventually realized that many times the reason for an attack of discouragement or depression is because God has great plans for us and the devil knows it and tries to short-circuit God's plan. This went on and off for several months. I loved the Lord with all my heart. I was reading my Bible, praying and committed to serving Him, but I was living the defeated Christian life in my thoughts and emotions. I didn't know what to do. As time went on, the Lord began to show me what I was dealing with and His strategy for being set free from the blues.

Over the years, I've had many wonderful opportunities to be depressed and disappointed. Just like you, everything has not gone my way. I've had to exercise more patience and endurance than I had planned on, I've failed at things, I've been misunderstood, unappreciated, and excluded at times because of my faith. The list goes on . . . great reasons for yielding to the temptation to be bummed out.

I've had big, honkin' pity parties and no one but me and the devil showed up! I've spent time seeking the Lord for His help when feelings of depression and disappointment tried to wrap their ugly arms around me. In the end, the Lord has helped me to see from His Word His plan for staying free from the blues. Victory over depression and the blues is possible. By operating in God's Word, I have experienced more days full of joy than depression. I laugh more than I cry. I see the cup half full rather than half empty. You can too! God's Word is rich in His wisdom for overcoming the blues.

❧**Nugget**❧   I realize that some of you may be facing more severe causes and types of depression. If you've lost a loved one, experienced divorce or a tragedy of some kind you may be in a time of heartbreaking grief; if you're feeling overwhelmed and anxious, or if you've experienced some type of traumatic stress you may feel like a prisoner to the oppressive power of depression. The Bible tells us to, *"Rejoice with those who rejoice, and weep with those who weep." Romans 12:15, NKJV* There are times to weep and mourn and we need to comfort one another in these times, but I believe that God's Word teaches us that He wants the majority of our lifetime to be filled with rejoicing after those times of grief and mourning. In Ecclesiastes 3:4, the Bible talks about *". . . a time to weep and a time to laugh, a time to mourn and a time to dance . . ." NIV* There is a time for weeping and mourning, but this will not envelope the rest of your life. Be encouraged to know that the time to laugh and dance will come. After a loss or tragedy people often feel guilty if they laugh or dance and they almost become locked in a prison of soberness and sadness. Certainly, there is a "time" for weeping and mourning, but God wants most of your lifetime to be spent in fullness of joy. Our focus in this study will be on joy, rejoicing, laughing, dancing and helping to lift you out of the season of weeping and mourning. Jesus said, *"Blessed are those who mourn, for they will be comforted." Matthew 5:4, NIV* This encourages us that a time of comfort will always follow mourning. I especially like the way The Message Bible paraphrases this verse: *"You're blessed when you feel you've lost what is most dear to you. Only then can you be embraced by the One most dear to you." Matthew 5:4, The Message* In the midst of being sad, grieving, mourning and facing discouragement and depression, be encouraged to know that as you keep your heart open to the Lord you will be embraced by the One most dear to you, Jesus Himself, and the Holy Spirit, your Comforter. After your time of grief and mourning, He will help you laugh and dance again, and it's my prayer that this Bible study is an encouragement to help you get there.

In this study we are going to focus our attention on general principles from God's Word for experiencing the life of joy and peace. Fortunately, God knows you and your circumstances intimately and He's sent the Holy Spirit to be your Helper, Counselor and Comforter. As you purpose to study and obey God's Word on this subject, expect the Holy Spirit to lead and guide you into a customized plan for freedom from depression in all of its forms.

Depression & Discouragement Is Epidemic

Commercials and advertisements for mood-enhancing drugs like Prozac®, Paxil® and Wellbutrin® bombard us on television and in print. They obviously have a big market, both with adults and children. The National Institute of Mental Health (NIMH) posted this on their website (http://www.nimh.nih.gov/nimhhome/index.cfm) *"Research has shown that in the United States about 19 million people—one in ten adults—experience depression each year, and nearly two-thirds do not get the help they need.*[1]

≈**Nugget**≈ When I conducted an Internet search on "depression", 15 million resources were at my fingertips in 5 seconds. Most sources said that depression is twice as common in women as in men. Everyone deals with a certain degree of feeling blue just because of normal life experiences. The loss of a loved one, continual stress caused by financial pressures, a business or marriage failure, uncertain economy, health or family problems can cause differing degrees of sadness. When these blue feelings begin to interrupt your normal ability to function for an extended time period and in a greater intensity, it's time to recognize the potential for a more serious problem that must be treated in some way.

Most experts agree on the basic symptoms of depression which include:

- *Persistent sad, anxious or "empty" mood.*
- *Loss of energy, interest or pleasure in activities, including sex.*
- *Diminished ability to enjoy oneself.*
- *Restlessness, irritability or excessive crying.*
- *Feelings of guilt, worthlessness, helplessness, hopelessness and pessimism.*
- *Sleeping too much or too little, early-morning awakening.*

- *Appetite and/or weight loss or overeating and weight gain.*

- *Decreased energy, fatigue, feeling "slowed down".*

- *Thoughts of death or suicide, or suicide attempts.*

- *Difficulty concentrating, remembering or making decisions.*

- *Slowed or fuzzy thinking.*

- *Persistent physical symptoms that do not respond to treatment, such as headaches, digestive disorders and chronic pain.*

Just what is depression? The NIMH says, *"Life is full of emotional ups and downs. But when the "down" times are long lasting or interfere with your ability to function, you may be suffering from a common, serious illness— depression. Clinical depression affects mood, mind, body, and behavior."*[2]

Depression can be caused by many things: genetic factors, biochemical factors, environmental factors, life stress factors, personality and social factors, life season factors, relationship and work factors, premenstrual, postpartum and menopausal factors, cultural factors, abuse and victimization factors, poverty, sickness and disease, and a blatant spiritual attack from the devil.

Without getting too introspective, describe a time in your life when you felt oppressed by depression or discouragement.

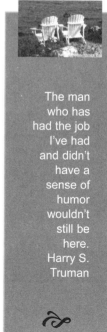

The man who has had the job I've had and didn't have a sense of humor wouldn't still be here.
Harry S. Truman

_____

_____

⮞**Nugget**⮜ The medical and mental health professions are doing their best to provide treatment for those affected by the blues. The most commonly used treatments for depression are antidepressant medication, psychotherapy, or a combination of the two. We thank God for the innovation He has given to medical science in this area. Sometimes these treatments help people, at least temporarily. Ultimately, if we want lasting results and authentic change we must put our trust in the Lord. God offers us supernatural help with the promise that joy and peace can replace depression and discouragement.

Join me as we take a journey in God's Word to find out what He says about overcoming depression, the blues, "the mentals and the bluks."

A Spirit of Heaviness

1.   Isaiah 61:1-3

In this passage, underline the words that describe depression and the blues.

1 The Spirit of the Lord GOD is upon Me, Because the LORD has anointed Me To preach good tidings to the poor; He has sent Me to heal the brokenhearted, to proclaim liberty to the captives, And the opening of the prison to those who are bound; 2 To proclaim the acceptable year of the LORD, and the day of vengeance of our God; to comfort all who mourn, 3 To console those who mourn in Zion, o give them beauty for ashes, the oil of joy for mourning, the garment of praise for the spirit of heaviness; that they may be called trees of righteousness, the planting of the LORD, that He may be glorified. NKJV

Another way of describing depression, the blues or being bummed out is by the phrase "a spirit of heaviness." Sometimes a person just feels heavy emotionally, mentally, physically and even spiritually. God wants us to be free from a spirit of heaviness.

What does God tell the poor?

What does He do for the broken hearted? _____

_____

What does God want for those held captive? _____

_____

What does He want for those in prison? _____

_____

What does He do for those who mourn? _____

What does He give in place of ashes? _____

What does He want for the spirit of heaviness? _____

God understands the reality of the blues, depression and a heavy heart. He realizes that these things make us poor, brokenhearted, captives, prisoners, mournful, covered with ashes and heavy hearted, and He provides freedom from all of these things.

Can you relate to any of these things? If so, describe it: _____

_____

2.   Acts 10:38

Underline the phrase "oppressed of the devil."

How God anointed Jesus of Nazareth with the Holy Ghost and with power: who went about doing good, and healing all that were oppressed of the devil; for God was with him. KJV

What did God anoint Jesus with? _____

What did Jesus do? _____

Did He leave anyone out? _____

What do you think it means to be oppressed of the devil? _____

In what ways is depression an oppression? _____

_____

Do you believe Jesus is still going about doing good and healing <u>all</u> who are oppressed by the devil?

_____

The good news is that although Jesus is not on the Earth today physically, He is still alive and healing and freeing people from all oppression, including depression.

3.   Hebrews 13:8

Underline the words "yesterday," "today" and "forever."

Jesus Christ the same yesterday, and to day, and for ever. KJV

Has Jesus changed? _____

If He did something good yesterday, would He do it today? _____

How long is Jesus the same? _____

⮞**Nugget**⮞ Jesus is the same! If Jesus went about doing good and healing all that were oppressed yesterday, that means that Jesus is still freeing people from oppression today. Jesus sets people free through His Word and by His Spirit. Sometimes this comes instantly and people are supernaturally delivered from depression. At other times, Jesus sets people free by giving them Holy Spirit inspired ideas, knowledge or wisdom that leads them to do any number of things: change their eating habits, their environment, seek professional Christian counseling or medical help, set personal boundaries, better manage their interpersonal relationships, etc. Jesus shows us from His Word how to think and how to speak in such a way as to not only be free from the oppression of depression and disappointment, but to stay free and walk in joy and gladness.

If a sense of discouragement, the blues, being bummed out, depression, disappointment or a heavy heart has plagued you, you are not alone. God has the help you need, but sometimes it's encouraging to know that the challenge you are facing has also been experienced by other people who loved God.

Godly People Feel Depressed At Times

David expressed his heart before God throughout the Psalms, and he let us know that a sense of depression often assaulted him. His response was to pray and seek God for help. Listen to his cry in Psalm 143:7-8: *"Come quickly, LORD, and answer me, for my depression deepens. Don't turn away from me, or I will die. Let me hear of your unfailing love to me in the morning, for I am trusting you. Show me where to walk, for I have come to you in prayer."* NLT

1.   Psalm 42:3-11

       Underline the phrases "in the dumps," "crying the blues," "I'll be praising again" and "He puts a smile on my face."

       3 I'm on a diet of tears — tears for breakfast, tears for supper. All day long people knock at my door, pestering, "Where is this God of yours?" 4 These are the things I go over and over, emptying out the pockets of my life. I was always at the head of the worshiping crowd, right out in front, Leading them all, eager to arrive and worship, Shouting praises, singing

If there is hope in the future, there is power in the present.
John Maxwell

*thanksgiving — celebrating, all of us, God's feast! 5 Why are you
down in the dumps, dear soul? Why are you crying the blues? Fix my
eyes on God — soon I'll be praising again. He puts a smile on my
face. He's my God. 6 When my soul is in the dumps, I rehearse
everything I know of you, From Jordan depths to Hermon heights,
including Mount Mizar. 7 Chaos calls to chaos, to the tune of
whitewater rapids. Your breaking surf, your thundering breakers crash
and crush me. 8 Then GOD promises to love me all day, sing songs all
through the night! My life is God's prayer. 9 Sometimes I ask God, my
rock-solid God, "Why did you let me down? Why am I walking around
in tears, harassed by enemies?" 10 They're out for the kill, these
tormentors with their obscenities, Taunting day after day, "Where is
this God of yours?" 11 Why are you down in the dumps, dear soul?
Why are you crying the blues? Fix my eyes on God — soon I'll be
praising again. He puts a smile on my face. He's my God.
The Message*

The entire psalm is about the discouragement the psalmist was
experiencing.

What symptoms of depression do you see in this psalm?

_____

_____

What was the solution in verses 4-8, 11?

_____

_____

Have you ever had a conversation like this with God? I love David's
honesty—while he freely shared his heart and discouragement with the
Lord, he always reminded himself with what he knew to be true about
God and His goodness to him.

2.   Psalm 43:5

Underline the words "discouraged" and "sad."

Why am I discouraged? Why so sad? I will put my hope in God! I will praise him again — my Savior and my God! NLT

What did David ask? _____

To feel discouraged, depressed or down is not necessarily a sin, but to stay in the "mulligrubs" is not God's plan. He is our help and way out.

☙**Nugget**☙   Sometimes it's helpful when you're discouraged to discover and isolate the reason why. I've found that the enemy seems to know where we are weak. He recognizes our weak link and looks for a way to push our buttons and trigger our weaknesses to bring on discouragement. It's our job to strengthen those weak areas. For example, if the enemy knows that having patience is a weakness in your life, he will find ways to test your patience with the hope that you'll fall into depression and discouragement.

Have you noticed any areas of weakness in your own life? If so, describe the way the enemy tries to capitalize on that area.

_____

Can you isolate any particular reasons that you feel blue? _____

What two things did David say "I will" do?

_____   _____

☙**Nugget**☙   Hope and Praise are two of your best weapons against the blues. When our hope is deferred, it makes the heart sick. God wants us to hope. We have to do it by faith. Hoping in God and His Word gives you the blueprint for a better future. To stir up your hope, remind yourself of "what can be . . ." Rehearse your dreams. Praising God is your next step of faith; praise God for what you know to be true, even when your feelings and circumstances are contrary. Praise the Lord for Who He is. Praise the Lord for all that He has done. By faith, praise the Lord for all that He will do and you will sense His Presence filling your life.

3.   1 Kings 19:1-21

In this lengthy passage, underline all the things God said to Elijah, who became very depressed as he faced persecution from his enemies Ahab and Jezebel.

1 And Ahab told Jezebel all that Elijah had done, also how he had executed all the prophets with the sword. 2 Then Jezebel sent a messenger to Elijah, saying, "So let the gods do to me, and more also, if I do not make your life as the life of one of them by tomorrow about this time." 3 And when he saw that, he arose and ran for his life, and went to Beersheba, which belongs to Judah, and left his servant there. 4 But he himself went a day's journey into the wilderness, and came and sat down under a broom tree. And he prayed that he might die, and said, "It is enough! Now, LORD, take my life, for I am no better than my fathers!" 5 Then as he lay and slept under a broom tree, suddenly an angel touched him, and said to him, "Arise and eat." 6 Then he looked, and there by his head was a cake baked on coals, and a jar of water. So he ate and drank, and lay down again. 7 And the angel of the LORD came back the second time, and touched him, and said, "Arise and eat, because the journey is too great for you." 8 So he arose, and ate and drank; and he went in the strength of that food forty days and forty nights as far as Horeb, the mountain of God. 9 And there he went into a cave, and spent the night in that place; and behold, the word of the LORD came to him, and He said to him, "What are you doing here, Elijah?" 10 So he said, "I have been very zealous for the LORD God of hosts; for the children of Israel have forsaken Your covenant, torn down Your altars, and killed Your prophets with the sword. I alone am left; and they seek to take my life." 11 Then He said, "Go out, and stand on the mountain before the LORD." And behold, the LORD passed by, and a great and strong wind tore into the mountains and broke the rocks in pieces before the LORD, but the LORD was not in the wind; 12 and after the wind an earthquake, but the LORD was not in the earthquake; and after the earthquake a fire, but the LORD was not in the fire; and after the fire a still small voice. 13 So it was, when Elijah heard it, that he wrapped his face in his mantle and went out and stood in the entrance of the Cave. Suddenly a voice came to him, and said, "What are you doing Here, Elijah?" 14 And he said, "I have been very zealous for the LORD God of hosts; because the children of Israel have forsaken Your covenant, torn down Your altars, and killed Your prophets with the sword. I alone am left; and they seek to take my life." 15 Then the LORD said to him: "Go, return on your way to the Wilderness of Damascus; and when you arrive, anoint Hazael as king over Syria. 16 Also you shall anoint Jehu the son of Nimshi as king over Israel. And Elisha the son of Shaphat of Abel Meholah you shall anoint as prophet in your place. 17 It shall be that whoever escapes the sword of Hazael, Jehu will kill; and whoever escapes the sword of Jehu, Elisha will kill. 18 Yet I have reserved seven thousand in Israel, all whose knees have not bowed to Baal, and every mouth that has not kissed him." 19 So he departed from there, and found Elisha the son of Shaphat, who was plowing with twelve yoke of oxen before him, and he was with the twelfth. Then Elijah passed by him and threw his mantle on him. 20 And he left the oxen and ran after Elijah, and said, "Please let me kiss my father and my mother, and then I will follow you." And he said to him, "Go back again, for what have I done to you?" 21 So Elisha turned back from him, and took a yoke of oxen and slaughtered them and boiled their flesh, using the oxen's

No person was ever honored for what he received. Honor has been the reward for what he gave. Calvin Coolidge

equipment, and gave it to the people, and they ate. Then he arose and followed Elijah, and became his servant. NKJV

In verse 1, what had Elijah experienced? _____

The prophet Elijah was tempted to be discouraged and depressed after a great victory. God's power had just been manifested and had blown away the Baal worshippers. You would think that Elijah would be flying high after this great ministerial success. Everyone except one woman thought Elijah was God's man. Jezebel hated Elijah and wanted him dead.

⊱**Nugget**⊰ It's interesting that often after a great success or a great time of consecration in life and ministry, we are most vulnerable to depression or discouragement. Hundreds of people can say, *"Praise the Lord, you did a great job."* And yet one "Jezebel-type" can be in the crowd and write you a nasty note, send you a critical e-mail or just get in your face and question your motives and purpose, and that one negatron will nullify all the good. Perhaps you just recommitted yourself to God and His plan and you've reached a new place of consecration, when suddenly you find yourself feeling the enemy's attacks on your confidence and abilities in an effort to get you down.

In verse 2, what did Jezebel want to do to Elijah? _____

In verse 3-5, what was Elijah's response? _____

In verses 5-8, how did God encourage Elijah? _____

Perhaps some of the first steps we need to take at times are simply improving our diet and rest. God used an angel to help Elijah eat and rest so that he could be strengthened.

What role does your diet or sleeping habits play in your sense of well-being?

_____

In verses 9-10, Elijah was discouraged again. What did he do and say?

_____

In verse 11-12, what did the Lord reveal to Elijah? _____

_____

The most important thing in life is hearing from and following God. When you're discouraged, it's a good idea to spend extra time with God in the Bible and allow His Word to saturate and marinate your mind. As you read the Scriptures, expect Him to speak a word in due season to your heart.

In verses 13-14, Elijah tried to invite God to his pity party.

Describe the pity party in your own words: _____

_____

In verses 15-18, how did God respond to Elijah's pity party?

_____

God barely acknowledged Elijah's whine! It's almost as if God disregarded it and just distracted him from his problem. God did let Elijah know that the premise that had him depressed was wrong and so he straightened out his thinking.

&**Nugget**& Notice that God put Elijah to work! I believe that the Lord knew when Elijah operated in the calling that God had for his life, he would be refreshed, so He immediately sent Elijah "back to work." There is something really healthy and energizing about operating in the gifts and callings God has in our lives. When we are not utilizing our God-given gifts, there is a feeling of dissatisfaction and unfulfillment. Often, we find ourselves depressed because we are not walking in the destiny, purpose and fullness of God's will in our lives.

We once talked to a gal that was gifted in organizational things. One day, as she was organizing an event, she made the comment that it just made her hormones happy to organize things. She was operating in her gift and it made her happy. When we operate outside of our gifts for an extended period of time we will feel empty and ineffective. I believe that there are multitudes of Christians that love God with all their heart, but they are not fulfilling God's plan for their lives. They have their own agenda and plans. Some of these people are very successful in business, the arts, medicine and in homemaking, but they struggle with depression and a sense of missing their purpose.

God knew that Elijah would find encouragement in fulfilling his destiny. I don't believe the Lord was being cold-hearted; He was trying to get some gladness flowing into Elijah's life!

In verses 19-21, what did Elijah do? _____

_____

☜**Nugget**☞ It's interesting that the end of this story has Elisha ministering to Elijah. God was going to allow Elijah to leave a legacy, and Elisha was the one God was using to bring that about. There is no better way to get out of depression than to get the focus off ourselves and onto others. Mentoring others and leaving a legacy is a great way to get our eyes off our issues and onto the needs of others.

Who's in your life that you can and should reach out to?_____

_____

Who are you mentoring? _____

What type of legacy do you plan to leave? _____

_____

Be encouraged if you've been tempted to have the blues, as we can see several of God's special people experienced the same thing. The good news is that it is God's plan to help you rise from the dumps!

Scriptures To Chew On

Taking time to meditate on and memorize God's Word is invaluable. Hiding His Word in our hearts will strengthen us for the present and arm us for the future. Here are two verses to memorize and chew on this week. Write these verses on index cards and carry them with you this week. If you will post them in your bathroom, dashboard, desk, locker or other convenient places, you will find these Scriptures taking root in your heart.

"How sweet are Your words to my taste,
Sweeter than honey to my mouth!"
Psalm 119:103, NKJV

"Yet in all these things we are more than conquerors
through Him who loved us."
Romans 8:37, NKJV

Group Discussion

1.   Describe a time in your life when you were blue, bummed or depressed. What factors contributed to that season? How did you communicate with the Lord?

2.   Describe the current culture and reliance on mood-enhancing drugs. Do you think there is an overemphasis on drugs? Do you believe drugs help people? What is your view on this?

3. Describe the role of diet, rest, work, stress, boundaries, your personal walk with the Lord and fulfilling your calling in terms of causing or curing symptoms of depression. Has the Lord led you to made adjustments in any of these areas?

---

[1]Robins LN and Regier DA (Eds). *Psychiatric Disorders in America, The Epidemiologic Catchment Area Study*. New York: The Free Press, 1990.

[2]Robins and Regier

Personal Notes

Personal Notes

No Pity Parties Allowed

Session Two

It would be nice if God would wave His "Tinker Bell" wand and sprinkle us with happy dust, wouldn't it? It would be great if we could click our heels like Dorothy and wake up joyful. The truth is that if we are going to be happy and joyful, we are going to have to start by encouraging ourselves in the Lord.

☙**Nugget**☙ I know this isn't what you want to hear, but the responsibility for your happiness is on you. It's not up to your mom, dad, husband, wife, children, best friend, the president, journalist or pastor. It's up to you! We must take responsibility for seeking the Lord and choosing His will. Often we look to everyone else to make us happy, only to be disappointed. We may need to lower the bar of expectation we have for others to make us happy. Perhaps we all have subtly put our hope in the happiness other people would provide for us, but we always find out that as wonderful and dear-hearted as our loved ones are, they cannot make us happy. It's not their job. It's very possible that God will use people to encourage us, but ultimately He wants us to be independently dependent upon Him and Him alone. If you've been the type of person that is continually disappointed with people, then it's time to do a 180 in your thinking. People will disappoint you. God will make sure of it, because He is a jealous God and He alone is to be the joy and rejoicing of our hearts! When our expectation is from the Lord and when we learn to encourage ourselves in the Lord, He will lead us to a place of great contentment and happiness and will often add God-breathed friendships into our lives.

Let's look at this subject of encouraging yourself.

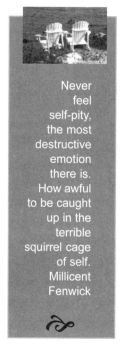

Never feel self-pity, the most destructive emotion there is. How awful to be caught up in the terrible squirrel cage of self.
Millicent Fenwick

Encourage Yourself

1.   1 Samuel 30:1-8

Underline the phrase "David encouraged himself in the Lord."

1 And it came to pass, when David and his men were come to Ziklag on the third day, that the Amalekites had invaded the south, and Ziklag, and smitten Ziklag, and burned it with fire; 2 And had taken the women captives, that were therein: they slew not any, either great or small, but carried them away, and went on their way. 3 So David and his men came to the city, and, behold, it was burned with fire; and their wives, and their sons, and their daughters, were taken captives. 4 Then David and the people that were with him lifted up their voice and wept, until they had no more power to weep. 5 And David's two wives were taken captives, Ahinoam the Jezreelitess, and Abigail the wife of Nabal the Carmelite. 6 And David was greatly distressed; for the people spake of stoning him, because the soul of all the people was grieved, every man for his sons and for his daughters: but David encouraged himself in the LORD his God. 7 And David said to Abiathar the priest, Ahimelech's son, I pray thee, bring me hither the ephod. And Abiathar brought thither the ephod to David. 8 And David inquired at the LORD, saying, Shall I pursue after this troop? shall I overtake them? And he answered him, Pursue: for thou shalt surely overtake them, and without fail recover all. KJV

David had left Ziklag and led his men to fight the Philistines. When they returned to Ziklag, they found the Amalekites had devastated their homes and families.

What happened to David and his people? _____

_____

Can you imagine the heartbreak and anger? Their homes and city were burned down, and their wives and children were gone; abducted and kidnapped. It was heartbreaking. Put yourself in their shoes. A great sense of despair and depression must have flooded their hearts.

What was their response to this tragedy?

_____

In the end of this passage, things went from bad to worse. Not only was David in turmoil personally, he became the scapegoat for everyone's pain.

In verse 6, what were the people talking about? _____

_____

What was David's response in light of this new threat? _____

_____

Encouraged: this means to strengthen, to prevail, to harden, to be strong, to become strong, to be courageous, to be firm, grow firm, to be resolute, to be sure.[1]

There are times when we just have to encourage ourselves in the Lord. We have to strengthen ourselves in God. We have to toughen up. Get some grit. Harden ourselves to despair and depression. We must make ourselves be resolute and courageous. It's not always easy, but it is required.

What do you think David did to encourage himself? _____

How do you encourage yourself in the Lord?

_____

In verse 8, what did David do? _____

Prayer is huge! When we seek the Lord and inquire of Him in the midst of tough times He directs and lifts us up.

No Complaining

1.   Philippians 2:14-15

Underline the things we are to avoid.

14 Do everything without complaining or arguing, 15 so that you may become blameless and pure, children of God without fault in a crooked and depraved generation, in which you shine like stars in the universe . . . NIV

When do we get to grumble, complain or murmur? _____

What does it prove when we choose to avoid the negative, pessimistic ways of thinking and talking?

_____

"Yeah, but what about (insert your specifics here)?" I can just hear some of you. *"Yeah, but you don't know my life or my boss or my spouse or my kids or my situation! I have a right to complain and murmur. Anyone in my shoes would do the same thing. It's just not possible to be happy and joyful in my situation. I have a right to feel like this!"*

That is a stronghold, my friend. It's a rotten way to view and live life. If we make a quality decision to rid ourselves of complaining, depression won't have anything to cling to. Let's not be like the whiney, spoiled children Jesus described.

2.   Luke 7:31-33

Underline the words "complain," "happy" and "sad."

*31 "How shall I describe this generation?" Jesus asked. "With what will
I compare them? 32 They are like a group of children playing a game
in the public square. They complain to their friends, 'We played
wedding songs, and you weren't happy, so we played funeral songs,
but you weren't sad.' NLT*

What did these children do? _____

Take Responsibility

1.   James 5:13

Underline the words that tell us the responsibility of the believer.

Is any among you afflicted? let him pray . . . KJV

What are you supposed to do if you are afflicted?

_____

Are you supposed to call the prayer chain and ask
everyone else to pray for you? Are you supposed
to lie down and have a pity party? No, the first
thing we are to do when we are afflicted is pray!
It's our responsibility to pray about our own
issues. Sure, after we have prayed it's great to get
others to agree with us, but <u>we</u> are to pray if we
are afflicted. It's our responsibility to pray for
ourselves.

What
God
expects
us to
attempt,
He also
enables
us to
achieve.
Stephen
Olford

2.   Isaiah 40:29-31

Underline the words "weak," "no might," "faint," "weary" and "fall."

29 He gives power to the weak, and to those who have no might He increases strength. 30 Even the youths shall faint and be weary, and the young men shall utterly fall, 31 But those who wait on the LORD shall renew their strength; they shall mount up with wings like eagles, they shall run and not be weary, they shall walk and not faint. NKJV

God gives power and strength to whom? _____

If we want our strength renewed and our spirits lifted up, what do we need to do?

_____

When we wait on the Lord, what is the result?

_____

How do you wait on the Lord? _____

_____

3.   Isaiah 52:2

Underline the phrase "shake yourself."

Shake yourself from the dust; arise, sit [erect in a dignified place], O Jerusalem; loose yourself from the bonds of your neck, O captive Daughter of Zion. AMP

After being in bondage for years, what did God tell the captives to do?

_____

Sometimes we need to grab ourselves by the back of the neck and shake off the oppression that the enemy tries to bring upon us. When you are tempted to feel sorry for yourself, stop and "shake yourself"! Don't allow discouragement and depression to keep you in captivity.

4.   Galatians 6:9

Underline the phrase "don't get discouraged."

And let us not get tired of doing what is right, for after a while we will reap a harvest of blessing if we don't get discouraged and give up. TLB

When you are encouraging yourself, don't get discouraged! You might not notice any difference in your life the first time you start to encourage yourself. If you've been down in the dumps for three weeks, it's going to take more than five minutes to move into a perpetual state of joy.

What does this verse tell us NOT to do? _____

What is promised? _____

What is our responsibility? _____

Are you ready to sow happiness and joy seeds into your own life? _____

5.   Jeremiah 30:19

Underline the phrase "depression days are over."

Thanksgivings will pour out of the windows; laughter will spill through the doors. Things will get better and better. Depression days are over. They'll thrive, they'll flourish. The days of contempt will be over. The Message

What happened to these people when God brought them out of captivity?

_____

Scriptures To Chew On

Taking time to meditate on and memorize God's Word is invaluable. Hiding His Word in our hearts will strengthen us for the present and arm us for the future. Here are two verses to memorize and chew on this week. Write these verses on index cards and carry them with you this week. If you will post them in your bathroom, dashboard, desk, locker or other convenient places, you will find these Scriptures taking root in your heart.

"Finally, my brethren, be strong in the Lord and in the power of His might."
Ephesians 6:10-11, NKJV

"Do everything without complaining or arguing,
so that you may become blameless and pure,
children of God without fault in a crooked and depraved generation,
in which you shine like stars in the universe . . ."
Philippians 2:14-15, NIV

Group Discussion

1.   Describe a time in your life when you looked to others for your happiness. Were you disappointed? What did you learn?

2.   Describe the way you encourage yourself in the Lord. What do you do to seek the Lord and find encouragement?

3.   Describe the importance of taking responsibility for the happiness you experience in life. Have you observed in your life, or the lives of others, the results of not taking this responsibility?

---

[1]The Online Bible Thayer's Greek Lexicon and Brown Driver & Briggs Hebrew Lexicon, Copyright © 1993, Woodside Bible Fellowship, Ontario, Canada. Licensed from the Institute for Creation Research.

Personal Notes

Personal Notes

Forrest Gump understood something: the importance of what he thought and what he said. "That's all I have to say about that" should be our motto! Both what we think and what we say are huge in determining whether we will have a life of joy or a life down in the dumps.

As we've already said, and as everyone who's ever read a health, women's or psychology magazine knows, the medical and mental health professions are doing their best to provide treatment for those affected by the blues. The most commonly used treatments for depression are antidepressant medication, psychotherapy, or a combination of the two.

Thank God for the innovation He has given to medical science and the help people have received through medication and therapy; but the question is, does God offer us His supernatural help with the promise of authentic results? Does God offer His supernatural help for overcoming depression and discouragement? Are drugs and psychotherapy the only options? Does the Bible reveal God's strategy for being set free from depression? The answer is yes! Depression, discouragement and disappointment are not God's highest and best. His best for us is a life of joy! Begin to imagine your life with a pep in your step, with a zig in your zag, with a glow in your flow! Life, the abundant life that Jesus came to bring, includes joy and freedom from depression, and God's Word tells us how to head in that direction.

Thinking like we (always) have is what got us where we are. It is not going to get us where we are going.
Albert Einstein

❧**Nugget**❧ Is it possible that God, through His Word, could do a work in our spirit, mind, emotions and even in chemical pathways of the human brain that would affect our behavior and disposition? Absolutely, with God all things are possible. As we cooperate with Him, His Word effectually works within us. Let's look at two important areas. What are you thinking? What are you saying? Your thoughts and your words will dictate your level of depression or joy.

What Do You Think?

The Bible is full of exhortations on what we think. Our thoughts determine our beliefs and our beliefs determine our attitudes and actions. It's a domino effect and it all begins with what we think.

1.   Philippians 4:8

Underline the words that describe the things we are to think on.

Finally, brethren, whatsoever things are true, whatsoever things are honest, whatsoever things are just, whatsoever things are pure, whatsoever things are lovely, whatsoever things are of good report; if there be any virtue, and if there be any praise, think on these things. KJV

What eight things are we supposed to think and meditate upon?

_____   _____   _____   _____

_____   _____   _____   _____

Is there any room in this verse for dwelling on depressing, sad, blue thoughts?

_____

Is there any place in this verse for being negative or for having a pity party in your thoughts?

Someone might say, *"Well, it's true. I am depressed and my life is a mess . . . and the Bible says to think on things that are true . . . so it's true, I'm depressed!"* Here's a question to consider: which is truer, your thoughts and experiences or God's Word? Think on the higher truth of God's Word and allow your mind to be renewed.

◈**Nugget**◈ Let's talk about "truth versus facts." This is so important. If we want to walk in the freedom God provides, we have to live by the truth. Often, the "facts" are contradictory to the "truth" found in God's Word. It may be a "fact" that we are bummed out and life feels rotten at the moment, but the "truth" of God's Word according to Psalm 118:24 is, *"This is the day the Lord has made and I will rejoice and be glad in it."* So, although it's a "fact" that I am bummed and discouraged; the truth is this is the day the Lord has made and I choose to rejoice and be glad anyway. Can you see the importance of choosing God's truth over symptomatic and circumstantial facts? This is what separates those who walk in victory from those who live in defeat. At times people feel that they are being dishonest or lying when they choose the truth over the facts. Don't let the voice of the accuser trip you up, choose the truth of God's Word in every situation and at all times. Facts are subject to change, truth is not. When the "facts" are not congruent with the "truth," we have to make a decision. Which one will we think on? Which one will we choose to act on? It's always wise to choose truth. Jesus said the truth will set you free. The "facts" will keep you in bondage. Sure, you may need to recognize the facts, but believe and act on the truth.

2.   2 Corinthians 10:3-5

In this passage, underline the things that come against our mind.

3 For though we walk in the flesh, we do not war according to the flesh. 4 For the weapons of our warfare are not carnal but mighty in God for pulling down strongholds, 5 casting down arguments and every high thing that exalts itself against the knowledge of God, bringing every thought into captivity to the obedience of Christ . . .
NKJV

When we are fighting a battle in our mind and emotions, we need weapons.

What kind of power do God's weapons have? _____

What three things do our weapons do?

_____ strongholds

_____ arguments and every high things

_____ every thought

What are we to do with our thoughts? _____

If you read this passage from the "bottom up", notice that everything begins with a thought, then moves into an argument or a high thing that is set against the knowledge of God and then finally that thought moves into a stronghold.

☙**Nugget**☙ Depression is a stronghold, but it doesn't start as a stronghold. It starts with a thought. For example, if we have the thought, *"I'm so bummed,"* and we don't take this thought captive and make it obey the Word, then this thought turns into an argument or high thing that goes against what God says. At this stage, we begin to argue for all the supporting reasons we are bummed out. *"After all, I have a right to be depressed. Look at my life! Here's the list of all the reasons I should be discouraged. I imagine that I'll always be depressed. God hasn't* *been fair to me. Where is He when I need Him?"* This argument or high thing then moves into a stronghold and we begin to get into the pattern of thinking, *"My life is such a mess. Nothing good happens for me. Who wouldn't be depressed? "* If we don't arrest those arguments and high things, then—voila!—we will have established a stronghold, and unless we do something about it we'll become a negative, pessimistic, depressed, blue person that no one wants to be around.

Can you see this progression? Thoughts move to arguments and high things and then they move to strongholds. The good news is that this sequence will work to establish a stronghold of joy in your life in the same way! For example, take a thought of joy and let it become an argument or high thing that agrees with God's Word; as you meditate and argue for this truth and imagine yourself full of joy, then in time joy will become a stronghold in your life! It's true.

3.   Isaiah 26:3

Underline the secret to enjoying God's perfect peace.

You will keep him in perfect peace, whose mind is stayed on You, because he trusts in You. NKJV

If we want perfect peace in our lives, what must we do with our minds and thoughts?

_____

How do you keep your mind stayed on Him? ____

_____

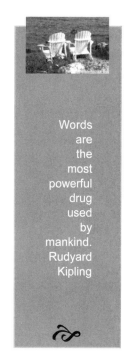

Words are the most powerful drug used by mankind. Rudyard Kipling

4.   Acts 26:2

Underline the phrase "I think myself happy."

I think myself happy, King Agrippa, because today I shall answer for myself before you concerning all the things of which I am accused by the Jews . . . NKJV

The Apostle Paul was a prisoner and falsely accused—he had a reason to be blue—and yet what did he tell King Agrippa?

_____

Paul could have said, *"This is so unfair. I am mad and this makes me sad. Why should I be a prisoner? I have nothing to say to you King Agrippa."* Paul chose to be happy because he understood what a privilege it was to be a witness for Jesus Christ!

What Do You Say?

What you say is what you get! It's true. Talk therapy is God's idea! He's given us one of the most incredible tools for joy, gladness and happiness and it's found just an inch or so below your nose! Our mouths carry power and it's vital that our words are congruent with our thoughts and in line with God's Word. Sometimes we feel like talking in a positive and uplifting way in agreement with God's Word, and sometimes we don't. If we want our Christian life to move off the emotional roller coaster, we need to say what God says—on purpose! Let's look at this.

1.   Isaiah 61:3

Underline the antidote for the spirit of heaviness.

To console those who mourn in Zion, to give them beauty for ashes, the oil of joy for mourning, the garment of praise for the spirit of heaviness; that they may be called trees of righteousness, the planting of the LORD, that He may be glorified. NKJV

What should we do if we want to replace "ashes," "mourning" and the "spirit of heaviness"?

_____

Praise is powerful! When was the last time you just lifted your voice at home, in your car, at church or anywhere to praise God in the midst of your discouragement? Praise God for Who He is and praise Him for what He's done for you. Do it today! Here's an assignment for you.

Write down twenty things you can praise God for. _____

_____

_____

_____

2.   Psalm 100:1-2

Underline the words "joyful shout," "gladness" and "singing."

1 Make a joyful shout to the LORD, all you lands! 2 Serve the LORD with gladness; come before His presence with singing. NKJV

How should we shout to the Lord? _____

When was the last time you shouted to the Lord with a voice of triumph? Why not do it, right now!

How should we serve the Lord? _____

How should we come before His presence? _____

Be honest. How many of us have served the Lord with madness? Sadness? We sometimes serve out of guilt, duty, obligation or martyrdom, but the Lord's plan is that we serve Him with gladness!

◈**Nugget**◈ It's pretty plain, right? Gladness comes with the territory. Anytime you find yourself mad, unglad, sad or bad when serving the Lord, something's not right. So, anytime you notice gladness lacking for an extended period of time, it's time to check your heart and find out what's up.

How do you serve the Lord with gladness when your feelings are contrary?

_____

Here are some additional suggestions for serving the Lord with joy.

First, you just choose it. You just choose to put on a happy face and say, *"This is the day the Lord has made and I WILL rejoice and be glad in it!"*

Second, you ponder your privilege. There is a great heart fulfillment that comes from knowing that your service to and for God is producing an eternal weight of glory! Ponder the thought . . . you GET to serve God with your life! You don't HAVE to, you GET to! How privileged we are to have been chosen by Him to bear fruit, much fruit, fruit that remains. That's enough to make us happy for the next few decades!

Third, think about the future. When this whole deal wraps up and you are face to face with the Lord Jesus—the Head of the Church—and He checks out your Daytimer to see how you spent your life . . . you are going to be happy that you served Him with gladness!

3. Psalm 118:24

    Underline the positive way we are to respond to each day.

    This is the day which the LORD hath made; we will rejoice and be glad in it. KJV

    Who gave us this day? _____

    What are we to do today? _____

4. Philippians 4:4

    Underline our responsibility to be happy!

    Rejoice in the Lord always. I will say it again: Rejoice! NIV

    What are we supposed to do always? _____

    Again? _____

    How do you rejoice? _____

    _____

    ❧**Nugget**❧ This is so simple, yet so huge. The last thing we feel like doing when we are down is rejoicing, right? I remember being in a job I didn't like and having a particularly bummer day. As I sat at my desk moping and complaining, I felt that the Lord spoke to my heart and said, *"Rejoice always."* I didn't feel like rejoicing. Again, the thought came to me, *"Rejoice always."* I really didn't feel like it, but I decided to do it anyway. So, in my sad, pitiful state I slouched at my desk and said, *"I'm joyful."* You

    Little faith will bring your soul to heaven, but great faith will bring heaven to your soul. Charles H. Spurgeon

couldn't tell it by my face or tone of voice, that's for sure! I said it again: *"I'm joyful."* This time I had a little more pep in my voice. I continued to say, *"I'm joyful"* several times and by the fifth or sixth time I said it, I started to laugh. That simple declaration of *"I'm joyful"* on a day when I was feeling bummed out lifted me right out of the bluks.

5.   Proverbs 18:21

Underline the two words that describe the power of our words.

The tongue has the power of life and death, and those who love it will eat its fruit. NIV

What part of you has the power of life and death? _____

What is your mouth producing for you? _____

What type of fruit are you eating in life? _____

Do you recognize this is the fruit of what you've been saying?

_____

This is for real. Have you been saying, *"I'm stressed? I'm worn out? I'm bummed?"* Or have you heard yourself saying, *"These kids are driving me crazy! My boss is ruining my life. I can't stand that waitress."* Blah, blah, blah!

Is it any wonder that people who talk like this are eating the fruit of a depressed, bummed out life? Change the way you speak! You can't go north (joyful) and south (depressed) at the same time, so make your decision and set your tongue like a rudder and head north!

⮞**Nugget**⮜   I have noticed something in my own life and in observing others. Just because we know some principles and truths from God's Word, that doesn't mean we are experiencing the resulting good fruit in our lives. Many people know they ought to guard their words and only speak words that edify and build up their own lives and the lives of those around them. Lots of people know they should not speak words that are counterproductive or contrary to God's Word, but the real proof of whether we know God's Word in truth is how much of it are we putting into practice. It's not enough to just "know" what the Word says. If you want to experience a life free from depression and discouragement and full of joy and gladness, you will have to "do" the Word. Don't be like the people who hear a truth from God's Word and say, *"Oh I already knew that."* Be the kind of person that honestly asks yourself, *"Am I doing it?"* According to God's Word, it's the <u>doers</u> of the Word that are blessed.

What phrases could you begin to say to turn your life in the right direction?

Scriptures To Chew On

Taking time to meditate on and memorize God's Word is invaluable. Hiding His Word in our hearts will strengthen us for the present and arm us for the future. Here are two verses to memorize and chew on this week. Write these verses on index cards and carry them with you this week. If you will post them in your bathroom, dashboard, desk, locker or other convenient places, you will find these Scriptures taking root in your heart.

"Death and life are in the power of the tongue,
And those who love it will eat its fruit."
Proverbs 18:21, NKJV

"Do not let any unwholesome talk come out of your mouths,
but only what is helpful for building others up according to their needs,
that it may benefit those who listen."
Ephesians 4:29, NIV

Group Discussion

1.   Describe how negative "facts" have robbed you or others from experiencing the "truth" of God's Word. Talk about the battle that is involved in choosing to think on the "truth" as more true than the "facts" of discouragement or depression you may face.

2.   Describe the process of something going from a "thought" to an "argument or high thing that exalts itself against the knowledge of God" to a "stronghold." Discuss this process in producing negative results and in producing positive results.

3.   Describe your life—the who, what, when, where, why and how of your lifestyle—as full of joy in 50 words.

Personal Notes

Personal Notes

It was a very stressful time in our lives. We were raising four young children, building a new church building and keeping up with the demands of a growing congregation. One day I noticed that I had not laughed in a long time. I consider myself a person who laughs easily and who usually finds the humor in just about anything, but for this season it was all work and no play, all serious and no laughter. I realized that I had gotten in a bad habit of not laughing!

To remedy the stress and seriousness that had overtaken my life I decided to start looking for the light side. I knew I needed to get a new vision so I searched through old boxes of photos looking for a snapshot of me laughing. When I found one, I posted that photo on our refrigerator so that I could get a new image of the person I wanted to be, again! It worked, and within a few weeks I found myself laughing and enjoying the season of life in a new fresh way. It was confirmed when a co-worker who heard me laugh one day said, *"I love hearing you laugh; you have not laughed in a long time."* How about you? Have you laughed lately?

With the fearful strain that is on me night and day, if I did not laugh I should die.
Abraham Lincoln

We've all had those days, weeks, perhaps long seasons where we just wanted to tune out all the negativity around us and run to our happy place. Well, here's good news: Jesus wants us to live in the happy place! Have you noticed that when you are full of joy, laughter and happiness in the Lord you are stronger in every way? You feel more energized. You are hopeful and motivated. The joy God gives us is our strength.

1.   Nehemiah 8:10-12

Underline the words "joy" and "mirth."

10 Then he said unto them, Go your way, eat the fat, and drink the sweet, and send portions unto them for whom nothing is prepared: for this day is holy unto our Lord: neither be ye sorry; for the joy of the LORD is your strength. 11 So the Levites stilled all the people, saying, Hold your peace, for the day is holy; neither be ye grieved. 12 And all the people went their way to eat, and to drink, and to send portions, and to make great mirth, because they had understood the words that were declared unto them. KJV

According to this passage, what is our strength? _____

_____

Why do you think the joy of the Lord gives us strength? _____

_____

Nehemiah told the people to rejoice in God's goodness. He told them to celebrate, change their thinking, eat feast foods and give gifts to others. A spirit of celebration accompanies the joy of the Lord.

In verse 12, what did the people do? _____

☙**Nugget**☙ Notice they made a choice to celebrate with joy! The King James Version of the Bible says they decided to "make great mirth." I love that! When was the last time you just decided to make great mirth? There is a lot of truth to the old song, "Don't worry, be happy." Joy is attractive. Joy is fun. Joy is refreshing. Often we have to stir it up and make ourselves rejoice.

Describe ways that you can begin to "make mirth." _____

_____

Whether it's small, natural things or big, spiritual things, we can make mirth. What refreshes you? What brightens your moment? What ways can you celebrate and stir up the joy of the Lord? Is it a thirty minute walk? Coffee with a friend? A new tube of lipstick or a fishing magazine? Is it alone time with God? Organizing a cluttered drawer? Shopping? A massage? Singing? Prayer and God's Presence? A funny movie? Watching the sunset? What is it for you? Make mirth!

 Nugget Here's an observation: In this story in Nehemiah when the people were wrongly interpreting the Word of the Lord, they were sad and depressed. When Nehemiah, Ezra and the Levites helped them to correctly interpret what the Word of the Lord meant, it brought great joy. Maybe you should take a moment to evaluate the things you are hearing. If you are reading books, listening to sermons or songs that are causing you to be overly introspective, depressed, sad and distressed, it's likely that those things are not in agreement with God's Word. Unfortunately, some preachers preach the Bible as if it were bad news. Certainly, there are some sober truths in God's Word, but for those walking with God in the light of His Word there is fullness of joy. Jesus said God's Word and His plan is Good News, and in most cases, good news brings great joy! Jesus Himself was anointed with the oil of gladness! I encourage you to take inventory of the things you are listening to or watching and be sure to read books, listen to music and sit under ministers who are preaching the Word in such a way that the truth you hear sets you free, and you experience the life and joy God's Word brings! God's Word is a delight and a cause for rejoicing in our hearts, if we will let it be. If you believe God's Word and take Him at His Word, it is absolutely thrilling!

2.   Psalm 45:7, Hebrews 1:9

In these verses, underline the anointing God endowed Jesus with. Circle the things we are to love and hate.

You love righteousness and hate wickedness; therefore God, Your God, has anointed You with the oil of gladness more than Your companions. Psalm 45:7, NKJV

You have loved righteousness and hated lawlessness; therefore God, Your God, has anointed You with the oil of gladness more than Your companions. Hebrews 1:9, NKJV

What was Jesus anointed with? _____

≈**Nugget**≈ Jesus was anointed with gladness. Too many people view Jesus as this sober, somber, serious person. No, Jesus had more joy than anyone else according to these passages. Isn't that awesome! He was not angry, sad, introspective, depressed or discouraged. I can just imagine Jesus walking around with a radiant joy and spirit of gladness as He talked with and ministered to people. Gladness is a sign of spiritual maturity.

Why did God anoint Jesus with such gladness according to this verse?

_____

3.   John 15:9-11, 16:23-24

Underline the phrase "your joy may be full."

15:9 As the Father loved Me, I also have loved you; abide in My love. 10 If you keep My commandments, you will abide in My love, just as I have kept My Father's commandments and abide in His love. 11 "These things I have spoken to you, that My joy may remain in you, and that your joy may be full." . . . 16:23 "And in that day you will ask

Me nothing. Most assuredly, I say to you, whatever you ask the Father in My name He will give you. 24 Until now you have asked nothing in My name. Ask, and you will receive, that your joy may be full. NKJV

Whose joy does Jesus want us to have? _____

How much joy does He want us to have? _____

What did Jesus say would give us His joy? _____

How would you define the phrase "your joy may be full"?

_____

_____

4.   1 Peter 1:8

Underline the adjectives that describe the joy of the believer.

You love him even though you have never seen him. Though you do not see him, you trust him; and even now you are happy with a glorious, inexpressible joy. NLT

As a person who believes and knows and trusts Jesus personally, what is our heart filled with?

_____

5.   Philippians 4:4

Underline the word that tells us when to be full of joy.

You don't stop laughing because you grow old; you grow old because you stop laughing.
Michael Pritchard

Always be full of joy in the Lord. I say it again—rejoice! NLT

According to this verse, when is it okay to be depressed? _____

To be full of the joy of the Lord, what are we to do? _____

_____

6.   Psalm 16:11

Underline the phrase "fullness of joy."

You will show me the path of life; in Your presence is fullness of joy; at Your right hand are pleasures forevermore. NKJV

Where do we find fullness of joy? _____

What is at God's right hand? _____

☙**Nugget**☙ God's Presence is a good place to hang out! You can tell who spends time in God's Presence because their life is marked by fullness of joy. After all, the Apostle Paul, inspired by the Holy Spirit told us, *". . . the kingdom of God is not eating and drinking, but righteousness and peace and joy in the Holy Spirit." Romans 14:17, NKJ* If you consider yourself to be a mature, spiritually developed person and your life is full of soberness, seriousness and a stoic disposition, you may want to spend more time meditating on God's Word and His promise of fullness of joy and gladness. Remember, Jesus was God's Son and He was anointed with the oil of gladness. When we spend time with God our Father, Jesus and the Holy Spirit we will find joy and gladness filling our hearts.

Laugh A Lot

Laughter is good for you! It's just impossible to be sad, depressed, bummed, blue or in the dumps if you cultivate a life of laughter. When was the last time you had a real hearty, refreshing laugh?

1.   Proverbs 15:13

Underline the thing that gives us a pretty face.

A happy heart makes the face cheerful, but heartache crushes the spirit. NIV

What does a happy heart do for your face? _____

_____

Want to look younger? Laugh! Happiness and joy light up your face!

2.   Proverbs 15:15

Underline the secret to a life full of feasting.

All the days of the oppressed are wretched, but the cheerful heart has a continual feast. NIV

What kind of days do those who are oppressed with depression have?

_____

What do the cheerful enjoy? _____

Notice, this is your choice! Which would you prefer: "wretched days" or a "continual feast"?

3.   Proverbs 17:22

Underline the result of a cheerful heart.

A cheerful heart is good medicine, but a crushed spirit dries up the bones. NIV

If you're thinking of being medicated for depression, have you considered this type of medication as well?

_____

The Message Bible makes it clear. *"A cheerful disposition is good for your health; gloom and doom leave you bone-tired." The Message*

What does a cheerful heart or a cheerful disposition do for you?

_____

What does doom, gloom and having the blues do to you? _____

_____

Everyone in medical science doesn't agree with God's Word on this subject. But there have been numerous people that have testified to the healing properties of laughter. Not all of these people have been Christians, but is it possible that they have tapped into something that the Lord told us in His Word thousands of years ago?

❧**Nugget**❧ An article on laughter and health that appeared on the website Howstuffworks says, *"We've long known that the ability to laugh is helpful to those coping with major illness and the stress of life's problems. But researchers are now saying laughter can do a lot more — it can basically bring balance to all the components of the immune system, which helps us fight off diseases . . . laughter reduces levels of certain stress hormones. In doing this,* *laughter provides a safety valve that shuts off the flow of stress hormones and the fight-or-flight compounds that swing into action in our bodies when we experience stress, anger or hostility. These stress hormones suppress the immune system, increase the number of blood platelets (which can cause obstructions in arteries) and raise blood pressure. When we're laughing, natural killer cells that destroy tumors and viruses increase, as do Gamma-interferon (a disease-fighting protein), T-cells (a major part of the immune response) and B-cells, which make disease-destroying antibodies. . . What may surprise you even more is the fact that researchers estimate that laughing 100 times is equal to 10 minutes on the rowing machine or 15 minutes on an exercise bike. Laughing can be a total body workout! Blood pressure is lowered, and there is an increase in vascular blood flow and in oxygenation of the blood, which further assists healing. Laughter also gives your **diaphragm** and **abdominal, respiratory, facial, leg** and **back muscles** a workout. That's why you often feel exhausted after a long bout of laughter — you've just had an aerobic workout!"[1]*

The psychological benefits of humor are quite amazing, according to doctors and nurses who are members of the American Association for Therapeutic Humor.[2] People often store negative emotions, such as anger, sadness and fear, rather than expressing them. Laughter provides a way for these emotions to be harmlessly released. Laughter is cathartic. That's why some people who are upset or stressed out go to a funny movie or a comedy club; so they can laugh the negative emotions away. These negative emotions, when held inside, can cause biochemical changes that can affect our bodies.

Here are some natural tips to help you put more laughter in your life:

- Figure out what makes you laugh and do it (or read it or watch it) more often. Funny movies, books and stories are a great source for priming the laughter pump.

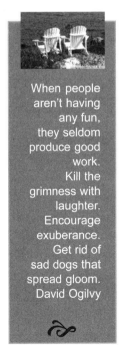

When people aren't having any fun, they seldom produce good work. Kill the grimness with laughter. Encourage exuberance. Get rid of sad dogs that spread gloom.
David Ogilvy

- Surround yourself with funny people—be with them every chance you get.

- Develop your own sense of humor. Look for ways to make others laugh. Find the light side and the bright side of every situation.

- Just start laughing and praising God, as a matter of choice on purpose. You'll be surprised by how refreshing it will be.

Norman Cousins' 1979 book, *Anatomy of an Illness*, brought the idea of laughter and healing to the forefront.[3] He was suffering from ankylosing spondylitis, a degenerative spinal disease which put him in almost constant pain. He decided to watch comedy films and laugh a lot. He discovered that as little as 10 minutes of laughter would give him 2 hours of pain-free sleep.

The explanation for why laughter reduces pain is not yet clear. While most people assume that it's because of the production of endorphins (one of the body's natural pain killers), there is still no scientific evidence to support this view. The reduced pain may also be explained by the muscle relaxation that occurs from laughter, or because humor and laughter distract us from the source of pain.

God knew all of this long ago when He told us that *"a merry heart does good like a medicine."* Make the choice to be joyful even in the midst of contrary circumstances and you'll be strengthened and lifted up!

4.   Psalm 126:1-3

Underline the words "dreamed," "laughter", "joy."

1 When the LORD brought back the captives to Zion, we were like men who dreamed. 2 Our mouths were filled with laughter, our tongues with songs of joy. Then it was said among the nations, "The LORD has done great things for them." 3 The LORD has done great things for us, and we are filled with joy. NIV

Has God ever released you from a captivity? Sin? Habits? Bondage?

_____

What is the automatic and courteous response when someone sets you free?

_____

If Jesus has freed you from any bondage then it is time to fill your mouth with laughter and songs of joy! Start declaring how good God has been to you and you will find His goodness overflowing into more and more areas of your life.

5.   Genesis 17:19

Underline the phrase "call his name Isaac [laughter]."

But God said, Sarah your wife shall bear you a son indeed, and you shall call his name Isaac [laughter]; and I will establish My covenant or solemn pledge with him for an everlasting covenant and with his posterity after him. AMP

What did God choose to name Abraham and Sarah's son of promise?

_____

Isn't that interesting? Through Isaac's name, God wanted us to be reminded down through the ages of His will for us to laugh and rejoice in the certainty of His promises! We have a friend whose nickname is Happy Hank and guess what? He's a happy guy! Being called Happy Hank every day, he's constantly reminded of living a life of joy. With a name like Happy Hank or in Isaac's case, Laughter, you just cannot be sad or depressed on a regular basis. Isaac, Laughter, cannot be sad. Happy Hank cannot live in depression. It's just not congruent. What do you call yourself? Let's hope it's not Grumpy, Dopey or Downer.

Perhaps you need to give yourself a joy-filled nickname and begin calling yourself Happy, Laughter, Joyful, Giggles, Bubbly, Smiley, Upbeat or Glad!

Sing A Song

Finally, let me mention the idea of singing "songs of joy." Singing songs of joy from your heart will do more to lift your spirit than just about anything. Did you know that you can sing songs out of your heart? As the Lord gives you words, just sing them out!

1.   Ephesians 5:18-20

Underline the words "sing/singing" and "song/songs."

18 Don't drink too much wine. That cheapens your life. Drink the Spirit of God, huge draughts of him. 19 Sing hymns instead of drinking songs! Sing songs from your heart to Christ. 20 Sing praises over everything, any excuse for a song to God the Father in the name of our Master, Jesus Christ. The Message

๑**Nugget**๑   Have you ever noticed photographs of people who are drunk? They usually look very happy, hilarious and joyful, right? When people are intoxicated with alcohol they often sing songs, laugh and act happy; the only problem is that it's a counterfeit to God's best. God wants us to enjoy the freedom, laughter and joy that comes from being drunk in Him. Get intoxicated with God and His Word. Living under His influence will fill your heart and mouth with songs of joy and gladness!

What are we supposed to drink? _____

What are we supposed to sing? _____

Where do songs originate within us? _____

≈**Nugget**≈   Hymns and spiritual songs don't have to sound like a dirge! God knows the style of music that will minister to your heart—it's not the beat or sound that is so important, it's the words! It doesn't matter if you sing songs that sound like country, R&B, rock and roll, rap or top 40; just sing words that are congruent with His Word from your heart! Step out and sing songs of praise and joy to the Lord from your heart. Make up the words as you go and you'll find that the Lord actually fills your heart and mouth with phrases and melodies!

2.   Psalm 126:5-6

Underline the phrase "songs of joy."

5 Those who sow in tears will reap with songs of joy. 6 He who goes out weeping, carrying seed to sow, will return with songs of joy, carrying sheaves with him. NIV

Perhaps as you and I pray and sow seeds of prayer, faith, giving and witnessing, there is a season of tears and earnestness. But what does God promise in the end?

_____

When we reap, what type of songs are we to sing?

_____

3.   Psalm 32:7

You are my hiding place; you will protect me from trouble and surround me with songs of deliverance. NIV

How would you describe a "song of deliverance"?

_____

> Some cause happiness wherever they go, others whenever they go.
> George Burns

≈

Why not make a decision to sing a song of deliverance from depression and discouragement? Let the Lord give you words from your heart and begin to sing them out by faith. You'll be blessed by the reality of deliverance!

Scriptures To Chew On

Taking time to meditate on and memorize God's Word is invaluable. Hiding His Word in our hearts will strengthen us for the present and arm us for the future. Here are two verses to memorize and chew on this week. Write these verses on index cards and carry them with you this week. If you will post them in your bathroom, dashboard, desk, locker or other convenient places, you will find these Scriptures taking root in your heart.

"Though you have not seen him, you love him;
and even though you do not see him now, you believe in him
and are filled with an inexpressible and glorious joy . . ."
1 Peter 1:8, NIV

". . . the joy of the LORD is your strength."
Nehemiah 8:10, NKJV

Group Discussion

1. Describe your "happy place." What do you do in your own personal life and walk with God to make mirth and find the place of joy, laughter and singing?

2. Give each person in your small group a nickname that describes joy, happiness and laughter. Be creative!

3. Find a photo of yourself laughing and post this snapshot in a place where you can view it on a regular basis. Share this photo with your small group and describe the circumstances of the photo.

[1] http://science.howstuffworks.com/laughter6.htm

[2] http://www.aath.org

[3] Cousins, Norman. Anatomy of an Illness. New York: W.W. Norton & Co., 1995

Personal Notes

Sing it!

"You've got to have frieeeends!" Bette Midler and Barry Manilow both told us so! Carole King promised we could lean on her, *". . . when you're not strong and I'll be your friend, I'll help you carry on . . ."* *"Just look over your shoulder honey, I'll be there . . .",* thank you Jackson Five! Carly Simon and James Taylor told us, *"Winter, spring, summer or fall all you have to do is call and I'll be there, yes I will, you've got a friend . . ."* Michael W. Smith reminded us, *"Friends are friends forever when the Lord's the Lord of them . . ."* Barbara Streisand summed it up, *"People who need people are the luckiest people . . ."* Are you one of those blessed people? Is friendship something you cultivate?

Do you remember all those songs? Three Dog Night had it right: *"One is the loneliest number!"* We need friends and good friends are a gift from God. As we mentioned before, the Lord wants us to be independently dependent upon Him as the source of our ultimate joy and encouragement. Jesus is our best friend, He sticks closer than a brother. He's our first love, but because He knows the value of godly relationships, He brings us together with people in His family in such a way that He provides divine, God-breathed, God-ordained, God-knit friendships.

It's amazing how lunch with a friend, a heartfelt e-mail, a funny card or just a simple word from someone who loves you can lift your spirit up right out of the doldrums.

Do not keep the alabaster boxes of your love and tenderness sealed up until your friends are dead. Fill their lives with sweetness. Speak approving, cheering words while their ears can hear them and while their hearts can be thrilled by them.
Henry Ward Beecher

God Knit Friends

1.   2 Corinthians 7:6

Underline the words "comfort/ed," "encourages/ed," "refreshes/ed" and "cheers/ed."

But God, Who comforts and encourages and refreshes and cheers the depressed and the sinking, comforted and encouraged and refreshed and cheered us by the arrival of Titus. AMP

What does God do for us? _____

What did the arrival of Titus, Paul's friend, do for Paul? _____

It's amazing how the right person at the right time can be used of God to comfort, encourage, refresh and cheer us up from the place of depression.

Who has encouraged you lately? _____

Who have you encouraged lately? _____

2.   Romans 15:30-32

Underline the thing that results when we have God-ordained relationships.

30 Will you be my prayer partners? For the Lord Jesus Christ's sake and because of your love for me-given to you by the Holy Spirit-pray much with me for my work. 31 Pray that I will be protected in Jerusalem from those who are not Christians. Pray also that the Christians there will be willing to accept the money I am bringing them. 32 Then I will be able to come to you with a happy heart by the will of God, and we can refresh each other. TLB

What did Paul need from his friends? _____

In verse 32, what did Paul say would happen for him and his friends when, by God's will, they were united?

_____

3.   1 Corinthians 16:17-18, 2 Corinthians 7:13

Underline the word "refreshed."

I was glad when Stephanas, Fortunatus and Achaicus arrived, because they have supplied what was lacking from you. For they refreshed my spirit and yours also. Such men deserve recognition. 1 Corinthians 16:17-18, NIV

By all this we are encouraged. In addition to our own encouragement, we were especially delighted to see how happy Titus was, because his spirit has been refreshed by all of you. 2 Corinthians 7:13-14, NIV

What does getting together with godly friends do for your spirit?

_____

4.   2 Timothy 1:16-18

Underline the phrases that describe the way Onesiphorus encouraged Paul.

16 The Lord grant mercy to the household of Onesiphorus, for he often refreshed me, and was not ashamed of my chain; 17 but when he arrived in Rome, he sought me out very zealously and found me. 18 The Lord grant to him that he may find mercy from the Lord in that Day — and you know very well how many ways he ministered to me at Ephesus. NKJV

Paul was facing persecution and discouragement. Describe the way Onesiphorus encouraged Paul.

_____

5. Philemon 1:7

Underline the words that describe the encouragement Paul received from his Christian friends.

For I have derived great joy and comfort and encouragement from your love, because the hearts of the saints [who are your fellow Christians] have been cheered and refreshed through you, [my] brother. AMP

A godly friend is a gift. What does a friend do? _____

_____

6. Exodus 17:12

Underline the key word that describes Aaron and Hur's help for Moses.

But Moses' hands became heavy; so they took a stone and put it under him, and he sat on it. And Aaron and Hur supported his hands, one on one side, and the other on the other side; and his hands were steady until the going down of the sun. NKJV

What role did Aaron and Hur play in helping Moses?

_____

Do you have a support system in your life? _____

List those friends who are in your support system: _____

_____

7. Proverbs 12:25

Underline one of the causes of depression and one of the cures.

Anxiety in the heart of man causes depression, but a good word makes it glad. NKJV

What does a good word do for us? _____

Who gave you your last good word? _____

8. Ephesians 4:29

In this verse, underline the type of words that are not encouraging.

Let no foul or polluting language, nor evil word nor unwholesome or worthless talk [ever] come out of your mouth, but only such [speech] as is good and beneficial to the spiritual progress of others, as is fitting to the need and the occasion, that it may be a blessing and give grace (God's favor) to those who hear it. AMP

What kind of words do we need to speak to others?

_____

What do such words impart?

_____

A supernatural deposit of grace is given to us when we choose to speak wholesome words that edify and build others up; grace to overcome depression.

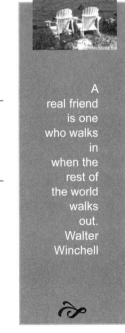

A real friend is one who walks in when the rest of the world walks out.
Walter Winchell

Scriptures To Chew On

Taking time to meditate on and memorize God's Word is invaluable. Hiding His Word in our hearts will strengthen us for the present and arm us for the future. Here are two verses to memorize and chew on this week. Write these verses on index cards and carry them with you this week. If you will post them in your bathroom, dashboard, desk, locker or other convenient places, you will find these Scriptures taking root in your heart.

> *"A man who has friends must himself be friendly,*
> *But there is a friend who sticks closer than a brother."*
> *Proverbs 18:24, NKJV*

> *"Reliable friends who do what they say*
> *are like cool drinks in sweltering heat — refreshing!"*
> *Proverbs 25:13, The Message*

Group Discussion

1. Describe some of the significant times in your life when friends encouraged and lifted you up.

2. Describe the importance of and challenges in having a support system. Talk about your current support system—what three people would you call on in a time of need? Are you a part of anyone's support system? In other words, who would call you?

3. Describe the importance of being in a small group and the ways you have found encouragement through one another.

Personal Notes

Personal Notes

You've heard it many times: *"Do unto others as you would have them do unto you."* Jesus said it and your mother drilled it into your ears. It's true. One of the best ways to find your own spirit lifted up is to lift up those around you. When we focus on meeting the needs of others it tends to distract us from our own issues and it puts things into perspective.

Encourage Others

1.   2 Corinthians 1:3-5

In this passage, underline the words "compassion" and "comfort."

3 Praise be to the God and Father of our Lord Jesus Christ, the Father of compassion and the God of all comfort, 4 who comforts us in all our troubles, so that we can comfort those in any trouble with the comfort we ourselves have received from God. 5 For just as the sufferings of Christ flow over into our lives, so also through Christ our comfort overflows. NIV

All compassion and comfort comes from whom?

_____

Has God ever comforted you in a time of trouble, disappointment or depression?

_____

If you want to lift yourself up, lift up someone else.
Booker T. Washington

We are carriers of God's comfort.

What are we to do for others? _____

What are some ways you can comfort and encourage someone who is down in the dumps?

_____

2.   Acts 4:36

Underline Barnabas' nickname.

Joseph, a Levite from Cyprus, whom the apostles called Barnabas (which means Son of Encouragement) . . . NIV

What was Barnabas' nickname? _____

Why do you think he earned this name? _____

If someone had to give you a nickname, what would people call you?

_____

3.   Romans 15:5-6

In this passage, underline the words that describe encouragement and harmony in relationships.

5 Now may the God of patience and comfort grant you to be like-minded toward one another, according to Christ Jesus, 6 that you may with one mind and one mouth glorify the God and Father of our Lord Jesus Christ. NKJV

What can we ask God to give us? _____

For what purpose? _____

Let's have the same heart to encourage one another that God has toward encouraging us!

4.   Philippians 2:1-5

In this passage, underline the way we should treat one another.

1 If you have any encouragement from being united with Christ, if any comfort from his love, if any fellowship with the Spirit, if any tenderness and compassion, 2 then make my joy complete by being like-minded, having the same love, being one in spirit and purpose. 3 Do nothing out of selfish ambition or vain conceit, but in humility consider others better than yourselves. 4 Each of you should look not only to your own interests, but also to the interests of others. 5 Your attitude should be the same as that of Christ Jesus . . . NIV

If we are united with Christ, we have plenty to be encouraged about!

How can we make the Lord's joy complete? _____

_____

What does verse 4 tell us to do? _____

5.   Ephesians 4:29

Underline the phrase "building others up."

Do not let any unwholesome talk come out of your mouths, but only what is helpful for building others up according to their needs, that it may benefit those who listen. NIV

What is one primary way we build others up? _____

Think about the words you say to others. It's an amazing thing to think of our words as carriers. They can carry life or death, blessing or cursing, encouragement or discouragement. We can build up or tear down. Put your mouth to work in lifting others up!

Friends Love Each Other

1.   1 John 3:11

Underline what we are to do for one another.

For this is the message that you heard from the beginning, that we should love one another . . . NKJV

What is God's message from the beginning? _____

2.   John 13:34-35

Underline the new commandment.

34 A new commandment I give to you, that you love one another; as I have loved you, that you also love one another. 35 By this all will know that you are My disciples, if you have love for one another. NKJV

How are we to love one another? _____

What will people see when we love one another? _____

3.   1 John 4:7-8

Underline the word "love."

7 Dear friends, let us love one another, for love comes from God. Everyone who loves has been born of God and knows God. 8 Whoever does not love does not know God, because God is love. NIV

What are we supposed to do for one another? _____

Who is the author of love? _____

If we are born of God—born again—what do we do? _____

4.   Romans 12:9-15

Underline the phrase "Love from the center of who you are."

9 Love from the center of who you are; don't fake it. Run for dear life from evil; hold on for dear life to good. 10 Be good friends who love deeply; practice playing second fiddle. 11 Don't burn out; keep yourselves fueled and aflame. Be alert servants of the Master, 12 cheerfully expectant. Don't quit in hard times; pray all the harder. 13 Help needy Christians; be inventive in hospitality. 14 Bless your enemies; no cursing under your breath. 15 Laugh with your happy friends when they're happy; share tears when they're down. The Message

What does the Lord tell us not to fake?

_____

What do good friends do?

_____

What are we to do when our friends are down?

_____

5.   1 Corinthians 13:4-8

Underline the word "love."

Sometimes our light goes out but is blown into a flame by another human being. Each of us owes deepest thanks to those who have rekindled this light.
Albert Schweitzer

4 Love endures long and is patient and kind; love never is envious nor boils over with jealousy, is not boastful or vainglorious, does not display itself haughtily. 5 It is not conceited (arrogant and inflated with pride); it is not rude (unmannerly) and does not act unbecomingly. Love (God's love in us) does not insist on its own rights or its own way, for it is not self-seeking; it is not touchy or fretful or resentful; it takes no account of the evil done to it [it pays no attention to a suffered wrong]. 6 It does not rejoice at injustice and unrighteousness, but rejoices when right and truth prevail. 7 Love bears up under anything and everything that comes, is ever ready to believe the best of every person, its hopes are fadeless under all circumstances, and it endures everything [without weakening]. 8 Love never fails [never fades out or becomes obsolete or comes to an end]. AMP

This verse separates the men from the boys. Loving others is a noble thought and we all want to be more loving, but 1 Corinthians 13 really makes it practical.

In what ways do you find you struggle with this passage? _____

_____

What area are you going to focus on improving? _____

_____

What does verse 8 promise you? _____

List the 25-27 different components to walking in love according to this Amplified version of 1 Corinthians.

_____

_____

_____

_____

_____

I encourage you to memorize this passage and make it your life mission. Jesus said the greatest commandment is to love God and to love our neighbor as ourselves, and 1 Corinthians tells us how to do it.

Make it your goal to be on the lookout for someone who needs encouragement and comfort. You can be used of God to help lift them out of the blues. Cry with those who are crying. Love them deeply. Speak words that will build them up. Have fun hunting for someone to bless!

Scriptures To Chew On

Taking time to meditate on and memorize God's Word is invaluable. Hiding His Word in our hearts will strengthen us for the present and arm us for the future. Here are two verses to memorize and chew on this week. Write these verses on index cards and carry them with you this week. If you will post them in your bathroom, dashboard, desk, locker or other convenient places, you will find these Scriptures taking root in your heart.

"Those who say they live in God should live their lives as Christ did."
1 John 2:6, NLT

"And as we live in God, our love grows more perfect.
So we will not be afraid on the day of judgment,
but we can face him with confidence
because we are like Christ here in this world."
1 John 4:17, NLT

Group Discussion

1.   Describe a time in your life when your encouragement lifted up another. What did you do to encourage this person?

2.   Describe the challenge of encouraging and lifting up those who are discouraged and depressed. How do you handle it when they do not respond immediately? What have you learned about being patient and consistent?

3.   Describe the power of 1 Corinthians 13. What one phrase in that passage challenges you the most?

Personal Notes

The "Bite Sized Bible Study Series"
By Beth Jones

When your words came, I ate them;
they were my joy and my heart's delight . . .
Jeremiah 15:16 NIV

- Six practical Bible studies for Christians living in today's culture.
- Each book contains 6 sessions designed for individual & small group study.
- Great studies targeting men, women, believers and seekers of all ages.
- Convenient size 6" x 9", each book is between 80-144 pages.
- Fill-in-the-blank book with Group Discussion questions after each session.
- "Nuggets" throughout each study explain Scriptures in easy to follow way.
- Written in a contemporary style using practical illustrations.
- Perfect for small group curriculum, bookstores and churches.

Satisfied Lives For Desperate Housewives
God's Word On Proverbs 31
Great Study For Women, Retail $7.99
ISBN: 1-933433-04-3

Session 1: Desperate For God
Session 2: Desperate For Balance
Session 3: Desperate For A Good Marriage
Session 4: Desperate For Godly Kids
Session 5: Desperate To Serve
Session 6: Desperate For Purpose

Grace For The Pace
God's Word For Stressed & Overloaded Lives
Great Study For Men & Women, Retail $7.99
ISBN: 1-933433-02-7

Session 1: Escape From Hamsterville
Session 2: Help Is Here
Session 3: How Do You Spell Relief?
Session 4: Get A Bigger Frying Pan
Session 5: Houston, We Have A Problem!
Session 6: Time Keeps On Ticking

Call Or Go Online To Order:
800-596-0379
www.valleypresspublishers.com

Kissed Or Dissed

God's Word For Rejection & Feeling Overlooked
Great Study For Women, Retail $7.99
ISBN: 1-933433-01-9

Session 1: Dissed 101
Session 2: Blessed & Highly Favored
Session 3: Edit Your Life
Session 4: That's What I'm Talking About
Session 5: Sow Acceptance Seeds
Session 6: Just Like Jesus

What To Do When You Feel Blue

God's Word For Depression & Discouragement
Great Study For Men & Women, Retail $7.99
ISBN: 1-933433-00-0

Session 1: When The Sky Is Not Blue
Session 2: No Pity Parties Allowed
Session 3: The Things You Could Think
Session 4: Go To Your Happy Place
Session 5: You've Got To Have Friends
Session 6: Lift Up The Down

The Friends God Sends

God's Word On Friendship & Chick Chat
Great Study For Women, Retail $7.99
ISBN: 1-933433-05-1

Session 1: Friendship Realities
Session 2: The Friendship Workout
Session 3: God-Knit Friendships
Session 4: Who's On Your Boat?
Session 5: Anatomy Of A Friendship Famine
Session 6: A Friend Of God

Don't Factor Fear Here

God's Word For Overcoming Anxiety, Fear & Phobias
Great Study For Men & Women, Retail $7.99
ISBN: 1-933433-03-5

Session 1: Fear of Death
Session 2: Fear of Man
Session 3: Fear of Danger
Session 4: Fear of Change
Session 5: Fear Factors - Peace & Love
Session 6: Fear Factors - Faith & Courage

Why The Gory, Bloody Details?
By Beth Jones

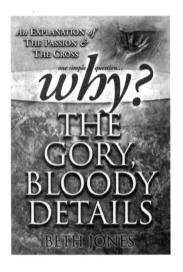

. . . right before
your very eyes–
Jesus Christ
(the Messiah)
was openly
and graphically
set forth
and
portrayed
as crucified . . .
Galatians 3:1, AMP

Why The Gory, Bloody Details?
An Explanation of the Passion and the Cross

Retail Paperback $4.99, Hardcover $7.99

ISBN: 0-9717156-6-1 Paperback
ISBN: 0-9717156-7-X Hardcover

This contagious 96-page giftbook answers the basic question, "Why did Jesus have to die on the cross?" People want to know: Why did Jesus endure such brutality? Why did God allow His own Son to be murdered? Why the gore and blood? It's a great evangelistic gift for unsaved friends and family and a great educational resource for believers who want to understand the cross and the passion.

- *Evangelistic gift book explains the cross—perfect for seekers.*
- *Gospel presented in a relevant, easy to understand way.*
- *Gift book size 4" x 6", 96 pages.*
- *Written in a contemporary style using practical illustrations.*
- *Hardcover and paperback.*

A Ministry of Kalamazoo Valley Family Church
995 Romence Road
Portage, MI 49024
Ph. 800-596-0379
www.valleypresspublishers.com

Beth**Jones**.org

a
simple
casual
blog

articles
and
bible
studies

topics
like
eternal life
girl stuff
healing
ministry
finances
holy spirit
prayer
victory
faq

click
it

.